PRAYERS

Without Knowing

God Was

Really There

VOL. 4

with

OSCAR DIXON

Pure Thoughts Publishing, LLC

Table of Contents

DEDICATION

Rev. Frank D. Dixon Mrs. Ethel M. Dixon

During my youth, I don't remember home life with an uncomfortable lifestyle; our parents had a harmonious relationship. I don't remember loud boisterous voices and disagreements coming through the house in the midst of seven children.

My innocence betrayed me as I grew older: what I was experiencing was not the norm in other homes; we had hard times, shortages of everything, but the love of our parents for us and the Lords, words can't describe.

My dad and mother were always hugging and playing with us, and I didn't know it then, but there were spiritual blessings of impartation placed on our lives. We grew up passing on to our children what we received from our parents, the Lord of their lives, is the Lord of our lives, and we believe the Lord brought the parents up the rough side of the mountain and set them on a solid foundation in Christ Jesus the Solid Rock, and so it is with us. I also dedicate these writings and testimonies to our parents and sisters and brothers; to tell the story is to be in concert with our upbringing.

PRAYERS

Vol. 4

Chapter One

PRAYER AND ANOINTING

Psalm 91:3:(niv) Surely he will save you

from the fowler's snare and from the deadly pestilence.

I have been talking to my prayer partners about attacks, a numbered of times others have requested prayers and anointing oil for cleansing and to help them learn how to defend themselves against spiritual attacks. The Lord teaches us the importance of praying the Word to overcome spiritual resistance to the plan of the Lord for our life. Spiritual attacks has been studied in our scriptures since the beginning of time, to help us stay strong in the Lord and have greater faith and victory over the enemy.

I heard it preached, when the evil spirits start interfering with your spiritual journey, it is primarily about your spiritual walk with Christ Jesus. He sends us into wilderness places, highway underpasses, park benches, and concrete beds seeking the lost and bringing them out of the darkness unto the marvelous light of the Lord. It is taught when we aren't being attached, is because we aren't making a big enough different in taking back the Kingdom of God, to help and prepare for the return of Jesus Christ for His Church. The Lord declares when He returns, His church will be without spot or wrinkle.

When we become that persons in our life we are ready to give our life to the Lord. We don't come by that decision lightly, often it takes years of being encouraged to belong to a Bible based church with teaching that will grow us. I can speak with encouragement and conviction, anyone who diligently seek the Lord they will learn of their gifts the

Lord has purpose for their lives and the "journey begins," learning how to walk in our calling through the Holy Spirit.

When you have given your life to the Lord, know that you have authority to use his name to come against the evil spirits that attack us, we must understand that we want the assurance of the Lord who is willing and able to go before us in this warfare, we must invite him into the battle and trust his leading and guiding us. Anoint your body from the crown of your head to the soul of your feet with oil, rejecting the evil spirits, declare the Holy Spirit has given me the Authority in this house, for I am the priest, I will cancel all evil forces by name and bind then in earth and in the heaven and lose the Spirit of Lord in the earth and in the heaven. Anoint yourselves inside and outside your homes declaring the blood of Jesus, to have all power over all that which is evil in Christ Jesus Holy name.

I will ask of the Lord to raise His hedge of protection over us and this house and all its family and possessions. To God be the glory, with Majesty and Power, is in His hand, and we are his creation, called into purpose, established by Him for Him.

TRANSLATION:

Psalmist, suggest very strongly, the Almighty God will carry us through all the dangers and fears of life. We must trade in all fears, and know that we trust the Lord and him only, to do this we must dwell and rest with him in spirit and truth.

Chapter Two

TRUST HIS COVERING

John 14:13; (niv) and I will do whatever you ask in my name, so that the Son may bring glory to the Father.

Early Friday morning I had a vision, I saw a partial face that I didn't recognize and the woman had her hair curl coming down the sides of her face. I was trying to get the best possible view to recognize the person, then I hear what I believe to be two knocks, the sound had a deep hearing a resounding that came closer. I pull myself from the bed and went to my prayer closet and began by inviting the Holy Spirit to lead me into the right prayer for this person's needs. I knew the Lord would pour in to my spirit what was needed, it is He who visited me in the spirit realm and with a knock He brought me to my feet.

I believe in praying immediately, the Holy Spirit is looking for a willing vessel He can pour out the prayers that is needed to bless his servant child in the name of our Lord and Savior. My desire to be obedient, I remember their have been many times I have called on Rapha my healer in the night watches needing and answer for myself or someone else. I am in expectation, hoping if the Lord call someone in the night watches to pray for me, they would pray immediately the Holy Spirit is trusting me with someone's issue, I must be obedient. I confess that I don't always get the assignment with the correct understanding, I asked the Lord to forgive my short coming and mistakes, I know my sins are against the Lord.

I said hello to my young friend in the afternoon, a few days later I explained to her this woman in my vision, I was not able to see her face clearly her hair was curled

 beautifully down the side of her face and this young friend exclaimed this is how she wears her hair. I felt the prompting of the Holy Spirit that she was the one, I said to this young friend, it is good the Holy Spirit loves you so much, He assigned someone to pray for you promptly and we continued to lament before the Lord that He would remember His Word.

I question this young woman, have you given your commitment to serve the Lord, have you come before the Holy Spirit and submit before Him whatever is required of you. She replied the Lord is very present with me, I am lead by the Holy Spirit even on my job. I receive assignments and visit the names He gives me, with this reply I felt the Lord presence and gave thanks.

Our prayer group leader called me shortly after I had talked with my young friend. I explained to her what had transpired and she said my friend's name came to her early this morning and she had been in prayer for her. Before we closed our prayer called we prayed mightily for her and other family members. My prayer is for the righteous, right hand of the Holy Spirit to deliver her well and protected in His righteous name.

Translation:

Jesus isn't saying the disciples would do more amazing miracles. He is saying working in the power of the Holy Spirit, would carry the gospel of God's kingdom out of Palestine and into the whole world.

Chapter Three

MY VISION

JOEL 2:29 (niv) Even on my servants, "both men and women, I will pour out my Spirit in those days.

This morning after scripture and prayer I laid on the floor and there came a most unusual vision. I seemed to have been in a huge old fashion church where I started in the basement with classmates from 1961. There seemed to be only a few of us there, they seemed to be working, no one seemed to notice me. There were candles all different colors burning beautifully and in array of lights that did shine bright.

The most unusual moving of the Lord became very presence in my spirit and my vision. It was almost unimaginable while walking through this basement in my vision, I see a conveyor belt with young people

placing boxes on the conveyor belts in the midst of all the bright lights. I recognized a few of my classmates while they were working. Today, I wonder was that and event for then or work in our future, that the Lord is planting a seed that He will nurture, and water until it is time for birthing. Over the years, in our class meeting when we had business segment discussion, I would on occasion received this warm and fulfilling presence. I would look around and see if anyone else were being affected like I was, with tears in my eyes.

This happen a number of times over the years, finally I spoke out in the meeting and informed our classmates. I told them, their have been a presence in my spirit when we have our class meeting. I informed them, I believe the Lord has something special for our class of 1961 to do. When we come together, He meets me hear and warms my spirit to tears, I don't know about others, this is a special love the Lord has for this class, as I pend to Him, His presence brought tears to my eyes. "Thank You Lord," I love You today.

I remember this spiraling object underneath me and it raised me up from the basement upstairs to the sanctuary. I notice the light up their was dim as I circle above the pews and finally I sit down on a pew behind a family friend on my right and another family friend on my left and the fire was coming of my hold body. Without touching my friends directly, I stretch-out my arms, this fire was going all around them as if there were a healing going on and my oldest friend seemed to be expecting it. He also asked me to do the person next to him on our right, when I moved my arms toward the man the fire hit him and he just fell up against the pew. I realized that I had to move so I went down the seat and others were getting the Holy Ghost fire and falling against the pews. There were other people in this large church with giant columns inside of it with a sizable congregation.

Somehow, I was back down stairs and everyone else had cleared out and I was picking up some items of mine.

I remember feeling very weak, I suppose all my energy were gone out, I collapsed to the floor. I don't ever remember staying in the spirit this long, and the first time I have ever been cover in the Holy Ghost fire of the Lord. Family, I haven't been able to determined what I was doing was the actuality of it, or perhaps the Lord showed me the works I should be doing and teaching others of "His Greater Works."

I do believe the Lord wants us out of traditional life styles and brought unto His transformative authority and powers to perform powerful acts through the Holy Spirit. Family, I was searching through meditation and commentary studies for a fuller understanding. Peter fell down but he didn't stay there, he met his friends afterwards in the upper room. When the Holy Spirit had come just as Christ had promise they went down from the upper room and laid hands on the people and preached the good news about our risen Savior many heard and believed, about three thousand were convicted and gave their life to Christ that day.

The Lord made it clear to me, He don't want to return for His church and find us making excuses, why you didn't do more in my name, I call you friend, therefore I told you what my "Father Told Me," make disciples.

I told Rev. Alphonso about this vision and how it occurred. It started in the basement of the church and went upstairs and were lifted up where I sowed over the benches and peoples and finally going back to the basement where the fire ended with all the lighted candles. He believed I were perhaps in the third heaven, whom the Lord leads and guides, He delights them as He pleases. This may be in the future.

TRANSLATION:

The outpouring of the Holy Spirit, promises to pour out on all flesh; and our sons and daughters shall prophesy and our young men shall see visions and the old men will have dreams. He will show us visions in the outer realms of heaven.

Chapter Four

TRUST YOUR PRAYERS

PSALM 34:8: niv) taste and see that the Lord is good, blessed is the man who takes refuge in Him.

Late this evening, I went down to my barn, the serenity is undeniably beautiful and the peace, I know the spirit of the Lord resides here, who else loves me enough to meet me here in my situation. I hadn't heard from my cousin since I was in New York, I was very concerned about her wellness. I came down to this barn because the Holy Spirit met me here one Sunday afternoon and I was in prayer to Him and desired an answer. Having prayed for a while and waiting, I resolve that my problem may not be as important as many others and decided to start up my truck and drive up to the house. The Holy Spirit called my name, "Oscar," with a voice, with clarity and power, with a vocal authority that I have never witnessed before.

I'll never forget that evening, I heard my name called from the heavenly realm, the sound of my name and the authority of that told me He is never to busy for them that are seeking Him.

I was humble immediately through my lack of thought forgetting for a moment in my distress that Our Almighty God is omnipotent, omniscience, and omnipresent and is never to busy to hear us call for Him and then He answers that let us know we have a personal relationship with Him. I didn't have one at that time, but I am going to seek Him until I can have that desire of my heart, a personal relationship with the Lord.

I have spent many days in personalized time in prayer, seeking the Lord and trying to better understand my purpose in life and meet health challenges that were arriving at that time. While praying at the barn I heard her name clearly along with two other names, I then began to pray for her with enthusiasm because she had been on my mind. My wife and I were with her in New York two months before. Since I came home, she hasn't answer or returned any of our telephone calls, the Holy Spirit speaks and I tried to obey by praying for her.

I asked the Lord to touch her heart when I call, that she would answer and this was a lesson for me to trust my prayers when I finish my prayers, I hear in my spirit, call her now and I did and she answered. We talked for a while, had prayers and I ask the Holy Spirit to bless and protect her, and we promised to talk more often.

Life trials will come at us, but don't quit, we have the Lord our God with us and He can do all things. We must trust that and keep our faith in the Lord.

TRANSLATION:

When sermons are preached, and prayers prayed, we here the offering to come and try this new walk of life. This is a warm invitation to try God; this is one of the first steps towards obedience in following God, we will discover, He is good and kind far this is two of the attributes of Christ found in The New Testament.

When we begin the Christian "life, our knowledge of God is partial and incomplete. As we learn to trust him daily, we will experience how good God is.

Chapter Five

YOU ARE NOT ALONE 1

Exodus 23: 25-26 (niv); Worship the Lord God and his blessing will be on your food and water. I will take away sickness from among you, and none will miscarry or be barren in your land, I will give you a full life span.

I was in my office, I received and emergency phone call from my cousin, and evangelist. She said, I am in my doctor's office I feel sick, something is happening to me. I understood she was having a health issue then she said cover me and hung up the phone. I said, if she called me, she must trust me because this was a powerful call for help, this call means she is depending on me, to call on our Lord, the Christ and His saving grace, I know He is the "Great Physician." I quickly realized the Lord had to give her my name and this realization gave me confident to come before the Lord and pray the bold, fervent and effectual prayer.

I went to the East window in my prayer quarters and asked the Lord to bless me with the right prayers for his daughter, my cousin, your beloved vessel Oh' God. I prayed to bind and cancel any and every attack that is trying to come against this beloved woman of the Lord. I am thankful for the Holy Spirit who knows what to pray for. I believe prayer and the doctors sustain her and they transfer her from the doctors office to the hospital, through the love and sustaining grace of the Lord.

The next morning, I took my friend and prayer partner to The Medical Center to visit her and learn of her health status. While waiting for the doctor, we began anointing her and praying and laying on hands in the weakened areas. The Evangelist moved for the first time according to the nurse, and whisper to me, "I received it." she moved and speaks, what a "Great God" Our Savior.

They relocated her to therapy for rehabilitation, I showed up one morning with more prayer warriors of faith, Deacon Hall and Rev. Frank Dixon, Boys. We took turns praying in depth and through the rewarding blessing of the Lord. She were smiling and moving her arm and fingers with smiles that were filled with tears. I was so thankful the Lord allowed me and others, to share in her blessing and healing.

Dear family, we have a takeaway, It does not matter what it looks like, whose report shall we believe, I will believe the report of the Lord.

TRANSLATION:

We are called to maintain a lifestyle that shows our faith. This can be a struggle, especially if our Christian lifestyle differs from the norm. Our lives should demonstrate that obeying God takes precedence over conforming to our neighbors' way of life. God's Word, not society, dictates how we should live.

Chapter Six

HE CALLS US TO PRAYER

I Timothy 2:8 (niv) I want men everywhere to lift
up holy hands in prayer, without anger or disputing.

I would dare to say it is better to be engaged to your
best friend than your boyfriend. When we have to
share times about our past life with one another, often
we share things that under ordinary circumstances we
wouldn't speak on those sensitive topics. We realize all
of us have a past, from truly understanding the Lord
blesses us as a friend in Him and a close friend that can
become a partner for life. Once you have jumped the
broom, spiritually speaking, The Lord have already given
us some keywords and enlightenment on how to handle

events and issues that come into our lives in our relation-ship.

"He Calls Us To Prayer," we are given the opportunity to come before him and receive training and discipline to go through preparation to get hitched at the altar. Pastor's give classes to shed light on what it looks like, and what to expect, we certainly need to be equipped to face our tomorrows. When a man believes he has found the right woman to have a future with and she feels the same way, I direct them to get counseling that provides an outline that each of them has a particular role in the marriage.

When I am to pray, I make every effort to be patient, invited the Spirit of the Lord into prayers, be led by the Holy Spirit to pray with bold, fervent and effectual prayer. It is the Lord who knows what we should pray for. Often we know the issues that surround the persons, only the Lord knows what and how we should come into our prayers, it is all about the Lord and He has established it so that all the praise and glory belong to the Lord.

I began praying for the family. The Lord was so present for me, and our prayers for the young family members. We were thankful as prayer partners. We can witness the improvement that prayer makes a difference, so this is why we lament before the Lord for full recovery continually for whomever the Lord has given us a name to pray for. I know this is done by prayer warriors of faith all the time. I welcome, many young folks and elderly that come to me more frequently and is in need of support and directions. Our Lord has already made the call, today this is a reminder because of the word. Galatians 6:9, And let us not be weary in well doing for in due season we shall reap, if we faint not."

We were pleased to pray and give these young couples desire to the Lord, that they would be blessed by him, who can do all things but fail. I pray that all marriages have longevity. There has been a grandmother brought to recovery from a period of downtime, another young lad gained clarity and balance in a full and beautiful way, his future outlook is very encouraging. There was a young man serving time, he had served half of his time and got into further trouble and would get additional time onto his sentence. Our friend and church deacon had an encounter with the young man family and they shared his story. The young man was sorrowful for this incident and is in prayer to the Lord, so please don't let the judge add time, he will straighten up and fly right, learn a better way of life, save him from additional time. Our deacon brought the request to the prayer team and we were convicted to do what Jesus did, he expected his disciples, friends, and followers to do. "As the Father has sent me, even so, I send you," (John 20:21.) "He who believes me will also do the works that I do. We prayed for the Lord to bless him, the Lord showed up and sit beside the judge and "said time served. "Our Lord wants to bless us, we are blessed and thankful to give the Lord all the praise and the glory.

TRANSLATION:

Besides displeasing God. anger and strife make prayer difficult. That is why Jesus said that we should interrupt our prayers, if necessary, to make peace with others. God wants us to obey him immediately and thoroughly. Our goal should be to have a right, relationship with God and also with others.

Chapter Seven

LEARN TO HEAR AND OBEY

John 15:8 (niv) This is to my Father's glory, that you bear much fruit, showing yourselves to be my disciples. There were five couples from our class of 1961, we were returning from vacation with our new found, best friends from outside of Kingston. We met these friends on a class reunion cruise from Seattle to Alaska couple years before. Enroute from our fantastic vacations which was to short for the weather and hospitality we enjoyed as guest. I was reading a powerful book written by Wade E. Taylor, The Secret of The Stairs this is an analogy of The Songs of Solomon.

While reading pages 80 and 81, I felt the prompting of the Holy Spirit so strongly, it brought me to tears. I was obedient to pray with all that was within me and for whatever reason, I was called to pray. My situation was complex at best. I was on a full flight from Kingston to Miami and I was trying to select a position to pray, because the fullness of the Holy Spirit was so fulfilling I could hardly breathe with tears flowing heavily down my cheeks from under my sunglasses. While I were reading, in the spirit, I saw a young woman walk down the aisle of the plane, she look at me with tears in her eyes. I didn't recognize her and I was called to prayer, I leaned forward on the passenger seat and began to pray. Perhaps the passengers wonder what's up with this guy crying like this, my wife knew something was going on, but what.

At the time, I knew not why to pray, when I arrived at the Miami International Airport, while waiting for my out outbound flight, I checked my cell-phone for messages. I received calls from our prayer team Leader , I told her about the vision and my being prompting to pray.

Later when I had arrived home, I was talking to our prayer team Leader, I explained to her the vision I had on the airplane when I was reading. The Holy Spirit showed me a young woman walking down the aisle of the plane, she turned and looked at me with tears flowing down her cheeks and I didn't know who she was.

Prophetess Frankie quickly said this is our friend's daughter. I immediately called her and talked to her, and received the full understanding. At the time I received the unction to pray and to pray boldly, fervently and effectually. I learned that a family member were having a serious accident, and was able to survive the accident. Our lessons in this is to be obedient to the unction of the Holy Spirit, in some instances we may never know whom we prayed for, but pray with all that is with in you, remember the Lord beckon us.

Today, I read this pending and felt the Holy Spirit presence. As I start this pending, the thought came to me maybe the presence of the Holy Spirit meant that I should pray like I did the last time, I have responded in prayer to the Lord and without ceasing.

TRANSLATION:

When a vine bears "much fruit,"God is glorified, for daily he sent the sunshine and rain to make the crops grow, and constantly he nurtured each tiny plant and prepared it to blossom. God is glorified when we develop a right relationship with him and began to "bear much fruit" in their lives.

Chapter Eight

AT THE CAR WASH

John 17:21 (niv), That all of them may be one, Father, just as you are in me and I am in you. May they also be in us so that the world may believe that you have sent me.

I try all ways to give the day to the Lord, He knows exactly what awaits each of us in our daily movement. I was uptown to the hand car wash, having my car detailed while sitting in the waiting room I see this woman in deep conversation with the cashier person and it seemed the person were having prayer with her perhaps. Another attendant walked up and this woman began to speak over his life and to give him prophecy from the Lord. While she was speaking to the second attendant, I felt the presence of the Lord strongly, I heard he need to choose better surroundings and get involved with things for his good, I believe it was said the Lord wants to help him grow.

I thought I heard, "you are next", that quiet, fulfilling voice could only be the Holy Spirit who knows all things. I was sitting, then got up, she released the young man's hand. Then came over, spoke, and reach for my hand. She looked at me very sternly and said "hello man of God," you have been busy doing the work of the Lord, I feel strongly the Lord is pleased with your service for others. Thank you I've been downtown in the streets of Atlanta for 13 or 14 years hoping someone would hear a word from the Lord and be released from their poverty, and bondage and fall into the arms of our Lord and Savior the Christ and be saved. He is working on your issue for you, He will bless your health and you are operating in a higher level of ministry for the Lord, as in the Apostolic Ministry.

I heard in the spirit she has been called into the ministry of the Lord, I said to her you have been call before into the ministry by the Lord. This time, I am going to call you in His name and anoint you to teach and preached the gospel and for Him that was crucified. Do I have your permission to anoint you to continue your work in mission ministry and the Lord is saying he wants you in a house to work for Him as well? She acknowledges she was raised up in the

Apostolic Ministry and working continually where ever she is lead by the Lord. She said when I spoke a word over her I cleared her from the enemy attacks, thank you Lord. was told by the attendant my car was ready, on the way out I explained to the second attendant that the prophet was speaking blessing over his life, and I hear in the spirit read your bible and start now in the Psalms 91, every night and the Lord wants you to write to Him, the desires of your heart, He is the one who provides, if we believe and trust the Lord.

TRANSLATION:

Our Lord especially prayed that all believers might be as one body under one head, animated by one soul, by their union with Christ and the Father in him, through the Holy Spirit dwelling in them. The more they dispute about lesser things, the more they throw doubts upon Christianity.

Chapter Nine

A TOUCH FROM THE MASTER

I Tim. 2:21; If a man cleanses himself from the latter, he will be an instrument for noble purposes, made holy, useful to the Master and prepared to do any good work.

My friend called from out of town and said his friend has a serious issue and he wanted me to pray for her. I called my prayer partner Prophetess Johnson, we pray often for others, she and I lifted her up in prayer. We put forth a powerful prayer for healing and good health. When we had ended Prophetess Johnson said

The Holy Spirit said He has it. When I read this I felt the presence of the Holy Spirit again.

That night, my friend and I called his friend and we prayed again. In that prayer, I felt the presence of The Holy Spirit, He wanted her to know the Holy Spirit said that there was a calling on her life and to seek Him.

On Tuesday, I was down at my barn in prayer for a revelation in reference to her health issue. I felt His presence when I wrote this. I often go to my barn, because I have had unusual experiences while at my barn in the presence of The Holy Spirit. While down at the barn, I was seeking insight and revelation from The Holy Spirit, whether this young woman would be healed outright or through an operation.

I went from my barn to the house, the phone rang, my cousin, The Evangelist was on the line. She says "I have a word from the Lord for you. He will heal her through her faith in Jesus Christ". When I heard that prophetic word, I was overcome and convicted by the blessing for the healing. I remind you,

I was at the barn praying for the answer, I went up to the house, my phone ring with the answer.

A great deal was happening on a phone call. The Evangelist asked me to pray for her when it was done. I felt this spiritual anointing go out to her and there would be a greater authority coming upon her, her levels of authority will increase according to the will of the Holy Spirit.

Since 2008, This Evangelist has received her license to preach the gospel and brings powerful prophetic words from the Lord as a prayer warrior, intercessor, and minister.

Such testimonies will do that which The Holy Spirit has a purpose for her. I was so thankful He allowed this vessel of the Lord to bring forth this anointing on his daughter.

TRANSLATION:

Don't settle for less than God's highest and best. Allow him to use you as an instrument of His will. You do this by staying close to Him and keeping yourself pure so that sin and its consequences do not get in the way of what God could do in your life. While God can redeem any situation, how much better it is to stay close to Christ and ready to be used by Him at a moment's notice.

Chapter Ten

THE LORD IS IN HIS GLORY

Colossians 1:28: (niv) We proclaim him, admonishing and teaching everyone with all wisdom, so that we may present everyone perfect in Christ.

CHRONICLES

1. Our family member called today and said she saw my face in her dream before daybreak and she got out of bed and went into prayer. That Wednesday night we prayed together

and the present of The Lord was very powerful and I received the healing.

2. A young man Charles was working on the landscape and he told me when he realized it, that he had gotten very hot and sat down and began to talk to someone he rarely talks with. I asked who was it, and he pointed up. I said very good, he saved your life from what you are telling me and The Holy Spirit showed up. He began to cry as I prayed blessings upon him. I said, "this Is the time to give your life to Christ." and he agreed. (9/8/10 14:00)

3. My friend came by Sunday afternoon to say hello. I hadn't seen him for a few days and I told him, I had been down in West Palm, Florida and The Holy Ghost had moved in a powerful manner of healing. As we talked I felt The presence of The Holy Spirit and I said I felt a prompting of Spirit to pray and anoint him, head and hands. This was a powerful anointing from The Holy Spirit and doing this

session, I thought I felt the urging about a house of God for him. This could be me desiring this for him, So I prayed as if it already were. (9/8/10 16:30)

4. I went to the Health Clinic, in West Palm, Florida for rest and recovery, but the Lord had planned my works already. On Tuesday, the health director was reviewing my health report and I felt the prompting of The Holy Spirit to place and anointing on the new institute, I asked her permission to anoint the two new facilities. She readily agreed and this was done. A few days later I blessed the director with the anointing and all those that will walk in the facilities will be blessed especially so when they walk into the facility the healing begins.

I was preparing for a lymphatic massage with the therapist and as she began, I felt the prompting of The Holy Spirit to anoint her with authority and healing and to speak and teach with authority. She invited me to her church and after service, she introduces me to her lady pastor, and The Holy Spirit prompted me to pray a blessing over her and to speak prophecy of her advancement in ministry. She will have more authority and

Her prayers will be more penetrating to the hearer.

5. The Holy Spirit had His way because there were others that The Holy Spirit prompted me to pray for. I and three men were walking after dinner and the Holy Spirit prompted me to pray and these men confess their well being and were amazed at how this had transpired. A lady was there for rest and recovery because she was emotionally and physically drained. Our God knows all our needs. He spoke through His servant and could see the weight of the enemy fall from her. I confessed we need to avoid carrying our burden when we have a God who is willing and able

because He tells us He is meek and kind and His burden is light and leave all our cares to Him.

These testimonies are Chronicles on how the Holy Spirit is moving in my life, and in these events. He demonstrates His word are supreme and will not return to Him void. All the praises and honor belongs to Him who trust this servant with His word for others.

TRANSLATION

In our scripture studies, the word perfect means mature or complete, not flawless. Paul wanted to see each believer matured spiritually. To experience these changes we must allow ourselves to be led by the Holy Spirit, when gaining that spiritual maturity, we know it is of God. Aside from the Holy Spirit, we can do nothing. We will have the power of God working in us as we grow daily motivated by love and not fear or pride, knowing that God gives the energy to become mature servants.

Chapter Eleven

THE AFRICAN REGIONS DELEGATION

Genesis 1:29; kjv.) And God said, Behold, I have given you every herb bearing seed, which is upon the face of all the earth, and every tree, in the which is the fruit of a tree yielding seed; to you it shall be for meat.

I received a call from the secretary to the official person of a major city, they had received my name and number from a friend. This call was to request support from the family tour company for service to support a mission trip. This African

Delegation came into the Country from several countries out of the African Region. I spoke to the leading official of the city, he wanted transportation support for The Africa Delegation that would travel through several cities in South Alabama. I was spiritually moved when asked to joined the delegation,

I felt the presence of the Lord when this request was made, I thought it was a remarkable opportunity to be involved in this mission ground-breaking event through several cities and discover what are they looking to accomplish that high officials have arrived. This delegation tour had a powerful implication for the future of several cities throughout South Alabama and other states that could benefit from the initial drive to draw support to participate in this economic development and cultural exchange. If this first undertaking drew the support needed to get this major project of the ground, what a blessing to be providing the opportunity to help put life back into our cities and breath the Lord's fresh breath that gives life into the nation. I believe our Lord wants this for us, I hope we are in great prayer continually.

The delegation had a meeting at a nearby hotel in the city on a Sunday afternoon, June 20, 2010. As the meeting progress, I realized this African region wants to become self-sufficient. They want to develop there own intra-structure, with roads, plants, and factories. They want to stop other countries from taking their valuable resources, raw products far there very own, loading them on ships and leaving them out of the profits and without jobs and poverty-stricken.

Our Lord God must be in this plan, even if it doesn't come into fruition on this first mission trip it must come in the future.

The Lord says, if we believe what has been spoken and it seemed good for the people, we can declare and decree a thing to Him, He can deliver. These countries want to harvest, can, package and ship out their own finish products to States and Cities that they have a relationship with. and I will bless their efforts. I carefully said this to the official of the city, seeking his approval and permission to pray. When I began to pray, the presence of the Holy Spirit was very evident, and presence, as I prayed a blessing over all that we envision and everyone with like mind for success the Lord can provide.

They are realizing that so much of our heritage and history have been marginalized and distorted, we need this opportunity to get it right. The Delegation spoke of establishing museum abroad and at home so we can be the one who tells our story. Dear Lord I hear jobs, jobs are coming in your name, to the Lord be the Glory.

When the meeting concluded that evening this was spelled out in detail how these Africa Regions wants to forge a relationship with us, starting in one city and traveling into possible seven cities having a meeting with officials to encourage them to join the team and become part of future growth in each of our cities and states. We met with the leader, he supports jobs growth through import and exports into the south.

These cities and officials from the African Nations wanted to know if we can help them establish there intra-structure and be the receiver of there goods into one of the largest ports? When things were concluded, I felt the prompting of the Holy Spirit say "pray, and I would bless their efforts", I said this to the leader. The meeting was for the immediate dignitaries trying to document and record the agreement that would start communication between nations.

I woke early that morning around 3:00 a.m.

and began to pray, a vision came upon me through the Holy Ghost showing me how He would spread His hand over those countries, the hills, down into the valleys, up through the hilltops again. He would bless those nations if they remain faithful to the Lord and to Him only they must serve, if the Nations stop serving the Lord, He would withdraw His abundance from them. The vision of the great abundance of the Lord, that were promised. When I read the scripture it agreed with the vision. Genesis 1:29-31 the blessing to come and the Word of the Lord has spoken and we are to believe.

I had mentioned, that I should have been at the last meeting to bless the documents that were signed. This move of the Lord speaks volumes when the document was left on the tour bus by accident, the official had looked everywhere and didn't locate the documents, he called and explain his situation concerning the misplaced documents. I called our worker who had detailed the bus he had the documents, I informed the official, I had the papers I didn't open them, but I heard in my spirit the documents were meant to be left on the bus. The Lord meant for His servant would pray and bless and anoint those documents far the prophecy he had given his servant to pray that His blessing would be upon them. Finally while pending this to the Lord, His presence came upon me and reminded me, His promise still stands, he will provide what He prophecy to those nations out of the West African Delegation.

Translation:

Herbs and fruits must be man's food including corn, and all the products of the earth. Let Gods people cast their care upon him, and not be troubled about what they shall eat, and what they shall drink. He feeds his birds will not starve his babes.

Chapter Twelve

Spiritual Guidance of God

Isaiah 52:7 (niv) How beautiful on the mountains are the feet of those who bring good news who proclaim peace, who bring good tidings, who proclaim salvation who say to Zion, "Your God Reigns,"

The Holy Spirit of God will guide us into right places only if we trust Him to do this by giving Him the reigns. My young friend came to me earlier today and asked me a very important and necessary question. "Mr. Oscar, what kind of church should I attend?" I said, "I'm not certain, I tend to believe that

I would like to be in a setting that would provide me with a pastor that I can reach, a teaching ministry that will help me grow and become that which the Lord has purposed for your life. A small church often provides this setting, you will need to interview and see if ministries are there to support your growth."

As I was explaining this direction to my friend, supporting him in moving forward, and that the Lord will guide him into right places and position him with teachers and pastors that can help him get to his next levels. As I made these suggestions, I felt the prompting of the Holy Spirit that we are on the right path to grow, "Thank you Lord."

I explained to my friend what I heard in my spirit, that a small church with the ministries in place and a pastor that teaches you how to grow and to be a support to others. I said most importantly, your help to others will be the most rewarding and fulfilling work you will ever do.

With that, I had felt the prompting of the Holy Spirit and I felt that he had been pointed in the right direction. I asked him about his previous church and he said he grew up in a small church with his mother. I said I am getting from The Holy Spirit, this is where your mother grew up and now is a minister in the gospel of Our Lord Jesus Christ. Perhaps it is a good place to begin again with the right mindset you can realize real spiritual growth. You must be committed to the Lord. Call me or come by any time. I call you family now, so did the Lord, call me friend; I offer you friendship.

TRANSLATION:

God says that the feet of those who bring good news are beautiful. It is a wonderful privilege to be able to share God's Good News with others, his news of redemption, salvation, and peace.

Chapter Thirteen

HIS EVER PRESENCE HELP

Proverbs 16:3 (niv) Commit to the Lord whatever you do, and your plans will succeed.

While in a Community Church Education Class, the minister was speaking about having the correct character when we are planning to move into leadership positions in your church. This took place this evening in September when these statements were made.

The question the minister asked, "Can any of us, make a difference here? Will we ever be in a leadership position?" On this statement, I felt the presence of the

Holy Spirit very strongly. A few years ago, at a friend's funeral, the minister was preaching the eulogy and stated in all his years preaching, he had not been in this pulpit, but the Lord had told him he would. He was, preaching the eulogy for this family, the presence of the Holy Spirit was very strong on me, almost to tears when that statement was made about coming to the pulpit in The Community Church. This was frightening, to say the least, going from the pew into the pulpit, but I do have confidence, under the guidance of the Lord. and the Spoken Word from the Holy Spirit. His word will come to pass, it is a journey that is in progress.

Sitting through several classes, I felt very confident that I would be well prepared by our ministers to come to the pulpit and be that which the Holy Spirit has called me to become, to preach his gospel and proclaim the day of the Lord. I remind myself, the Holy Spirit has called me and the training is a process, this journey is an ongoing work, and I pray that the Holy Spirit continues to be upon me, as he guided me through this training to get my required documents to meet the obligations to preach in the pulpits and continue to work on boards . At this time, I have preached in that church three times and served on two separated boards over two years on one of them and more than seventeen years on another. The message here is to stay in prayer, seeking guidance from the Lord for the right direction, if the Lord calls you to ministry than He will equip you. He will set you before well-trained ministers and instructors, to help you get it right. When I have been assigned to bring the message, I felt confident, and thankful for the training help prepare me, and I went to The Christian Life school of Theology.

TRANSLATION:

There are different ways to fail to commit to whatever we do for the Lord. Some people commit their work only superficially.

They say the project is being done for the Lord, but in reality, they are doing it for themselves. Others give the task temporarily to the Lord when it isn't going their way, you take it back, and others give the task fully to the Lord, but lend no support for its completion or success and you wonder why we didn't succeed.

We must maintain a delicate balance, trusting the Lord fully as if everything depends on Him while working as if everything depended on us. You will learn to be led by the Holy Spirit and receive his encouragements and realize success in your completions.

Chapter Fourteen

LORD BE PATIENT WITH ME

Psalm 46:1 (niv) God is our refuge and strength, an ever-present help in trouble.

I have challenges with my health, that has been pressing upon me and I have not been working on assignments that the Lord had set before me as often as I should. With the health issue upon me and the need to work on my assignments, I am low on energy and feeling, will I get the health and strength to do my assignment?

When you feel the Holy Spirit pressing you to stay on your assignments, other issues come up and set roadblocks in such a way you know the devil is busy. So I am not a shame to call on the Holy Spirit for help, because, He promises to be our ever-present help when we need Him, and I said, "Right now Lord, I need your righteous hand to protect me in middle of my storms."

Early Sunday morning, as I woke, I started humming a few words to a song I don't know but is familiar with a few words that go like this: "Please be patient with me, the Lord is not through with you yet." In this, I received encouragement to stay positive and to further strengthen, the same day at my 11:00 a.m. service that was reiteration during my pastor's sermon. Truly the Lord speaks to our need if we stay in prayer with the Holy Spirit, regardless of what it looks like.

On Sunday night, my longtime friend and I come together for intercessory prayer and this began earlier this year of 2010. There was a lesson to be learned when we first began when all of the team isn't available the two of us pray just as committed. The joy in these testimonies, is the Lord put this upon my heart to do and if I received the Holy Spirit's message correctly, my friend is the team leader, I prayed blessings of the Holy Spirit upon him. While writing this, I felt The Holy Spirit of God and we will continue to be lead by Him.

My Big Brother had a praise report, on a young man that is incarcerated, we have prayed continually for him. The young man told my friend that he had been praying that when he goes before the judge, he asked the Lord to let him do the remainder of his two years and not let the judge add additional time. When the young man came before the judge, the judge looked at his documents and said,

I am going to set you free with time serve twelve months, as soon as they get your papers processed you are free to go.

I pray now in the name of Jesus Christ, that many others will be set free in their hearts and their cell doors will break open as they did for this young man.

TRANSLATION:

The psalmist teaches us to trust God at all times, if there were world destruction coming upon us, we are to trust God, no matter what. The psalmist expressed a quiet confidence in God's ability to save him. God is our refuge even in the face of total destruction. He is not a temporary retreat, He is our eternal refuge and can provide strength in any circumstance.

Chapter Fifteen

YOU ARE NOT ALONE III

Psalm 118:17; I will not die but live, and proclaim what the Lord has done.

There is this vessel of God that I come to know and she demonstrates that she is sold out for Christ Jesus. The first time I met her, she was on a mission sent by The Lord to go and pray for another servant, and while there, I met her and also had her to pray for me. That day, a new friendship was born and our steps have been ordered by the Lord and since today we have worked together as intercessors for others and also for our families and each other.

I remember the time she called me over four years ago and said she was coming up from out of town to see me at home and I gave her directions. When she arrived, we had prayer and in her prayer, she revealed to me that I was a soldier of the Lord and would be going on missions. This was an answer that I had been waiting for because there had been an announcement made in my church for volunteers for a mission trip months earlier and I couldn't answer because I had not received an answer from the Lord. The power of this Prophetess prayers that Saturday morning was overwhelming and fulfilling for answer prayers and direction that the Lord was pointing me toward. When Jesus walked upon the earth, He told his disciples to go and preach and teach in all the lands, spreading His glory upon the nations.

That evening the Prophetess drove from out of town to see me, you may remember her story about having had two major issues.

However, God not only sustained her but renewed her with the ability to walk and talk again and are also driving daily. On her second issue, the fight was greater, but the Prophetess was unyielding, praying from her stomach powerful prayers blessed by The Lord. Our Lord and Saviour called me to her bedside and revealed His authority to heal and deliver her from the second attack and she is now mobile using both arms and hands and is walking with a slight limp. She drove up from out of town, I knew when she arrived that afternoon that she had a word from The Lord.

Her speech was a little weak, she handed me a note that read: Proverb: 18:16 God has placed a Gift inside of his people (men) and (woman) when you come to know what Gifts, He has placed in you, start using your Gift, it will cause you to come before Great men. Healing, Teaching, Laying on Hands and Speaking Wisdom.

I declared and decree in this pending, those

who read and believe these testimonies that Our Lord and Savior heals, they will also receive the spiritual blessing of Our Lord. It is through our testimonies that others are made whole, for what He has done for her or me, He will do the same for you. We will proclaim victory today in the name of Jesus and tell others our testimonies and believe on the Lord Jesus Christ that they too will be made whole.

Our take away with this Prophetess is that she sacrifices for others, the battle is daily through the Lord. I am encouraged when I read about this "Woman of God," and so are you children of the Most High God, Believe in your heart He is the only one that can deliver and set us free through His saving grace.

TRANSLATION:

Each day we put our trust in someone are something, and don't give a great deal of thought or concern, whether it is safe or not. We demonstrate daily, airplane pilots and all other modes of transportation, we trust the driver. That being true, are we willing to trust God to guide us here on earth? While being led, we are going through character building, becoming more Christ-like each day undergoing a transformation as Kingdom Children.

Many dangers, seen and unseen, the Holy Ghost goes before us and covers us in so many situations and protects us. Even when some issues attack us, we so often don't get the full hit, because of the leading of the Holy Spirit.

Chapter Sixteen

ANSWERED PRAYER

Proverb 13:24: (niv) Whoever spares the rod hates their children, but the one who loves their children is careful to discipline them.

It's good to have neighbors that you can feel free to visit almost at any time, I roll up in their yard and knock on the door, I can tell they are genuinely glad to see me. I visited our elderly neighbor on a winter day, and the temperature would be cold that night. I drove up to say hello, I hadn't visited her since her friend passed. She invited me in and the room was cold, after a few minutes I asked her was the heat working, she replied that she called the heating service two days before. I asked, "Can I call the heating person and see what is the problem, you need heat in the house." The service answered I replied, "This is Oscar, I am visiting my neighbor, she needs heat, can you come today." After a little hesitation, he said, "Yes, I will see you soon." "Thank you," I replied. It is always good to be a blessing to someone else, only the Lord can lead and guide us into right places, He is glorified and won't forget kindness easily.

We had moved into our home a few months, a short time later a storm with high winds came up my driveway and tumble a couple trees directly across the road. My neighbor heard the crash, called me about the damage, and apologized he didn't have a chainsaw to cut the trees up so he could move them. Instead of my wife and I getting dressed for church, I went to my barn and retrieved my chainsaw and cleaned up the damage.

Thank you Lord for training me for the young man, the prayer seemed to be what he needed. He came up to the house on occasions, we had scripture with encouragement that he would do well in his future, just keep the Lord in his life.

"Mr. Oscar, will you be my mentor?" I reminded him he doesn't need a mentor, "I been visiting your parents for a few years, stay under the guidance and teaching of your mother and father you will have a bright future." This happened a number of times over the last few years, one day there was a knock on the door, my young friend greeted us with a bowl of homemade soup, made Irish style and cornbread and sat it on the kitchen counter. He gave me a hand made greeting card. When I read it, I was floored, it brought tears to my eyes, to me I'm just a caring neighbor such as yourselves who pray for me often. The card reads; Psalms 116:7, "The Lord hath dealt bountifully," Thank you for being a friend and mentor to our son,

I know you are a spiritual man when my son said he feels like he is talking to God whenever he talks to you! So thank you for your support and especially for your prayers for our family. Family, I am going to try and repeat this, my friend brought that greeting again with the homemade soup and cornbread, when I was under the weather she brought over a nut cake, I hadn't told them I was under the weather, ain't God good.

Family, our take away is, our young people are so impressionable today we need to provide the bread of life and what The Word taught us. We can witness and give testimonies through our experiences that represent what the Lord expects from us, to pray what He gives us and when we study The Word of the Lord. II Timothy 3:16, all scripture is given by inspiration of God and is profitable for doctrine, for reproof, for correction, for instruction in righteousness.

TRANSLATION:

It is not easy for a moving parent to discipline a child, but it is necessary. The greatest responsibility that God gives parent is the nurture and guidance of their children. The lack of discipline puts parents love in question because it shows a lack of concern for the character development of their children. Without discipline children grow up with no clear understanding of right and wrong and with little direction for their lives.

Chapter Seventeen

THE HOLY SPIRIT SPEAKS

Vol. I, 13 by FUCHSIA PICKETT

ACT OF ANOINTING; PAUL declared that his anointing was from God, "who also sealed us and gave us the Spirit in our hearts as a pledge"

I Corinthians 1:21: Now he which establisheth us with you in Christ, and hath anointed us, is God; 1:22: Who hath also sealed us, and given the earnest of the Spirit in our hearts.

He meant that God has made us like the

109

Anointed One, Christ Jesus in the sense that the same Spirit has anointed both Christ and us. I John 2:27, The Scriptures teach us that "the anointing which you received from Him abideth in you, and you have no need for anyone to teach you; but as the anointing teaches you about all things, and is true and is not a lie, and just as it has taught you, abide in Him."

A important characteristic of "Oil", it provides light when it burns in a lamp. In the Bible days, oil was the chief source of illumination, apart from the sun. That light symbolizes the power of the Holy Spirit to illuminate truth to us.

Jesus said, "I am the light of the world" The Holy Spirit filled Him and He walked as Light in the darkness of this world. Then He declared to His disciples, "Ye are the light of the world." Jn.8.12: Then spake Jesus again unto them saying," I am the light of the world: he that followeth me shall not walk in darkness but shall have the light of life.

"FIRE: In the scriptures, it typify the presence of God. When the children of Israel were in the wilderness, the presence of the Lord was with them in a cloud by day and a pillar of fire by night. Exodus 13.21; And the Lord went before them by day in a pillar of a cloud to lead them the way; and by night in a pillar of fire, to give them light; to go by day and night, from before the people.

Fire has power to destroy, but this is not why the Lord used to represent the Holy Spirit. The work of the Holy Spirit is redemptive, not destructive when under the control, fire is an invaluable element that provides warmth and light and it cleanses and purifies whatever it touches. The Scriptures teaches that "our God is a consuming fire" Hebrew 12:29; For our God is a consuming fire. His holiness is the essence of that fire.

TRANSLATION:

Our Strength and ability are owing to faith, and our comfort and joy must flow from faith.

Chapter Eighteen

SOWING SEEDS FOR HARVEST

Luke 15:1 (Niv) now tax collectors and sinners were all gathering around to hear him.

Today, I was at a Conference for our churches, this was youth day, the minister invited the young speaker to bring the message today. She charged our youth and the adults to be willing to change your lives and follow The Lord. We must be willing to go into the strongholds and preach and teach the word of God where ever it takes us. Don't be concerned what others think about you, just know that we are children of God at work winning souls for Christ obvious they knew each other. The elderly lady said, she felt well, but was losing weight and was going into the hospital this week to find out what is the problem. At that moment, minister Fran took her hand and began to pray for her, when she was about finish, I felt the presence of the Holy Spirit to declare her well, because it was already done in the name of our Lord and Savior the Christ, who gets all the glory today and be magnified.

I believe minister Fran shouted, "Yes" when I said it was already done because The Holy Spirit was very present, I was breaking down into tears. I walked away with the fired of God upon me, that means filled with the Holy Ghost. The Lord is calling us into His mission fields to preach the gospel, that means abroad into third world nations and our very own parks, street corners where the lost are seeking for the word of God.

TRANSLATION:

The very reason Jesus came is described by the type of people he associated himself with. Jesus risk defilement by touching those with leprosy and neglected to wash himself up in the prescribed manner. Naturally, the Pharisees were very clean with there rituals and avoiding others. Jesus came to offer salvation to sinners, to show that God loves them, Jesus didn't worry about the accusations. Instead, he continues going to those who needed him, regardless of the rumors concerning the type of people he associated himself with.

I am hoping, that we are not guilty of the same mistakes and attitudes of the Pharisees, and neglect the very souls that need to hear the good news of God.

Chapter Nineteen

"HE" SENDS INTO OUR LIVES

Micah 2:1-2: (niv) Woe to those who plan iniquity, to those who let evil on their beds! At Morning's light, they carry it out because it is in their power to do. V.2) They cover fields and seize them, and houses, and take them. They defraud people of their homes, they rob them of their inheritance: V.3) I am planning disaster against this people from which you cannot save yourselves. You will no longer proudly, for it will be a time of calamity.

I remember when I first heard this young minister's voice, I was in the process of purchasing our new home following my retirement. I was in the early stages of working at my local church I had joined recently, at that time my cell phone rang. This young pastor introduced himself, I didn't recognize the voice, then he tells me I worked with a good friend of his at my previous job before I retired. This was so unusual this young minister call me and had already called my wife. He prayed with her and now he would like to pray for me and whatever I stood in need of. I explained to him about the bank trying to prevent the purchase of our new home. This young pastor, who I knew not, brought forth this anointed prayer from own High that only the Lord could provide for that occasion. The prayer was so overwhelming it left me with fresh energy and thoughts on how to approach this attack.

I walked into the church office, got permission to use the phone and called the N.A.A.C.P. I explained the circumstances how my wife and I were trying to obtain our new resident, each time we neared the assigned closing date, they request new information, this time I said no more information, I realized, I needed help to obtain my mortgage closing. The attorney instructed me to give them a 24-hour ultimatum for a closing, or prove why I didn't qualify. The broker called the next day on the 21st hour, with a closing the next day.

Early that next morning I heard in my spirit, Micah 2:1-3." Family, I believe I dropped the ball on the scripture, I wasn't certain at the time I believed I was supposed to read the scripture at closing. I remembered family, I trusted what I heard, the Lord called this into existence, who shall stand in His pathway. To this, I say "Sweet Jesus and Darling Holy Ghost," my ever present help.

Just before I left home, my real-estate broker called to inform me the bank wanted more information for the closing, and they may request a new closing date. At that time when the young pastor called, I was parked on the church property preparing to renovate the playground, take out all the old rotten materials and replace it, and so it was done with courage and conviction the Lord would be pleased.

I recognized the bank was hard lining me, they were trying to find a reason to abort my purchase. My broker didn't recognize this hard-lining was racially motivated, in order to succeed in their attempt they needed to find me at fault. I assured myself the bank couldn't prevent my purchased the Lord had spoken to me in the night watch and told me "not to get comfortable," where I was at, he spoke earlier the day before I had planted new flowers and the lawn was

growing, and I received this warming presence as I walked across the yard. I heard in my spirit "don't get comfortable where you are at." I was confident in what I heard, I wasn't certain how the Lord would work this out, I am a believer I claimed the property for my wife and I.

I was accepted on the trustee board by the pastor, and shortly after they went forward with planning to renovate the learning center. There was major work to be done on the interior renovation for the learning center and the playground. Today, the learning center is striving with young families and is continuing to grow. To see the church today, from its humble beginning and the growth that has taken place and the multiple ministries and the forward planning that is going on, I can speak a word with great faith, this location was in the spirit of a "Visionary," Our Lord and Savior, the Christ only plant great seeds that He nurtures and waters. The vision given to the pastor, the Lord elevated to Bishop and he passes the continuation to the incoming pastor.

The Lord gave increase to the new pastor, with his leadership abilities new growth came and it was sustainable in the church and his arm wasn't short because he launched ministers from his staff to become pastors and also assist other churches also with ministers. The works that were already on the way, went forward in excellent renovating the sanctuary and flooring throughout. You can easily agree the hand of the "Lord has done this." I believe the Lord did say, servant, you have done well with the assignment I have given you. Practice what you have demonstrated in your next office as Bishop, there is much work to be done, that I will require of you.

TRANSLATION:

Woe to the people that devise evil during the night, and rise early to carry it into execution! It is bad to do mischief on a sudden thought, much worse to do it with design and forethought. It is great a moment to improve and employ hours of retirement and solitude in a proper manner. If covetousness reigns in the heart, compassion is banished; and when the heart is thus engaged, violence and fraud commonly occupy the hands.

Chapter Twenty

HE ANSWERS PRAYER

Psalms 65.5 niv) You answer us with some deeds of righteousness, O God our Savior, the hope of all the ends of the earth and of the farthest seas.

Our prayer team was established a few year ago by our younger brother who is no longer with us, the thought to have a prayer team came to his mind one day, I have no doubt the Holy Spirit put this desire upon his heart, he was obedient and call our oldest sister and shared this unique assignment.

Our brother was obedient and made the calls, the prayer team was established and put into existence. This didn't represent the beginning of this prayer team, we were prayer intercessors before then. We were brought together uniquely by the hand of the Lord having prayer through a chat line. His blessing was upon us, and the assignment we were involved in increased in names to pray for, hospital visits, nursing homes and taking the elder and others to hospitals or doctors appointment. We labored through our prayers for those persons, their situations, conditions, and all matter of illnesses the Lord sustained us and we witness recoveries and others came on the prayer line and gave their testimony. We acknowledged that our Lord deserves all our praise. He guided us into this one great voice coming up to Him, He assembles and establishes our going and gave us His authority to use his name in prayer, preaching and anointing, He would be in His

Word.

Earlier today, Prophetess Frankie called and followed up on our prayer and discussion from last night concerning my health and the insight the Holy Spirit gave her. Her prayers and support have been enormous, I thank the Holy Spirit for His great love knowing each of our needs and blessing them.

Prophetess Frankie called again tonight very concerned about the housing situation for our family member who has been waiting for his housing unit to be completed. It has not been done and they are heading into another winter. We all have prayed many months for the Holy Spirit to move and give us resolution because we are in expectancy.

Prophetess Frankie called, I was on her mind to ask my thoughts concerning our family member getting his housing unit completed, she wanted us to lend more prayer and meditation towards the contractor failing to complete units as agreed. I was in my office with my son, there was a warming presence of the Holy Spirit that began to speak in my spirit. I was surprised and amazed I was receiving information and understanding. I noted what I heard spoken to me, the developers abandon the project perhaps because of the new presidential installation and perhaps those pre-committed funds were in question. We encouraged our family member to pray and invite the Lord to guide him through these difficult times, to lead you and guide you in a new location if it's the Lord's will, or we will be patient and wait on the project of housing to be completed. If there is another area you would like to live, pend it to the Lord and take perhaps a day fast and your prayer family are in agreement and you have our support. Trust the Lord who loves the opportunity to be the first choice and the only choice for all our needs. With this approach it calls for trust and believe the Lord answers prayers. Trust in the Lord with all your heart and lean not on your own understanding, in all your ways acknowledge Him and He will direct your path. Family, we are called to a prayer life, seek me while I can be found, we are to remember, if we decrease coming to Him, we decrease his presence with us. This gives the increase, it gives me more courage to stay near the cross, for the Lord knows already what I'm standing in need of. I asked the Lord to let someone know Oscar needs prayer, back in the day I would call my sisters, or brothers or other partners. I asked the Lord and be patient, to my good and the Lord answered prayers I received texts, phone calls, get well cards in the mail, I read them and is drawn to tears, these people the Lord touched their heart with my name and they were quicken.

TRANSLATION:

Though sins fill our heart, you forgive them all, with dread and awesome power you will defend us from our enemies, O God who saves us. You are the only hope of all mankind throughout the world and far away upon the sea.

Chapter Twenty One

HOW CAN I SERVE

Psalm 1:6; (KJV) For the Lord knoweth the way of the righteous: but the way of the ungodly shall perish.

Today the weather is cold, the sun is becoming brighter and I give thanks to the Holy Spirit waking me up this morning and set my feet in the right places. I went to the Barbershop to get my facial trimmed.

My barber was anointed a few days ago when the prompting of the Holy Spirit led me to anoint her. After the anointing she was so thankful the Holy Spirit answered her prayers that she had been seeking answers. I asked what was the prayers for. She replied she wanted to do something for the Lord out of her shop because He has been blessing her. Through the anointing, she can move forward and pray and bless others when led by the Holy Spirit while working in her shop. He answers the question, "How Can I Serve? Become a righteous servant for the Lord and he will show you how.

Today, she gives me her testimony that transpired about three weeks ago when she informed the gentleman that wanted his beard shaped up, but didn't have enough money for both. As I was leaving, I paid for his beard shape up and informed her this was her first opportunity to pray and bless someone's life. Our barber tells me when she told the gentleman that he had a complimentary beard, he was so thankful that she realized that he was very short on funds, she then blessed him with a complimentary haircut and prayed blessing on his life. She tells me a few days later he returned, it seemed the Holy Spirit was

still upon him and he was thanking her for the blessing that was of the Holy Spirit. What seemed ordinary to pay for his beard shapeup and complimentary haircut from the house may seem ordinary, to the gentleman the Holy Spirit met his need, and grew his faith.

We who are called into the service of the Lord, believe that if he calls us, he will grow us into that prepared servant that He has already purpose for our lives, in serving Him. Our barber prayed for me today after finishing my shapeup, she said the Lord told her to pray and bless me and she did so.

At the nursing home today, I was praying for the patients, while reading Psalm 23rd, verses 1 through 3, I felt the presence of the Holy Spirit on verse three.

It reads, Psalm Chapter 1:3; And he shall be like a tree planted by the rivers of water, that in his season; his leaf also shall not wither, and whatsoever he doeth shall prosper. I thank the Holy Spirit for His patience for the nurturing and has continued to grow me each day and I am thankful.

TRANSLATION:

He is a blessed man, a happy man, and a righteous man, he avoids evil influences, deeds, and attitudes, he delights in God's Word. God will cause him to prosper, but the ungodly is worth no more than the chaff, his destiny is judgment. The Lord watches over all the plans and paths of godly men.

Chapter Twenty Two

HE WILL GROW YOU

PETER II 3:18, But, grow in the grace and knowledge of our Lord and Savior Jesus Christ. To Him be the glory both now and forever.

My young friend and I have known each other for a few years, over a short period I didn't hear from him, he called one day and informed me he was a new dad. His situation seemed good on the surface, when we talked, there were underlying issues.

In the midst of his issues, he had been talking to me about his prayer life, and he believes he could feel the presence of the Holy Spirit at times but didn't know what it meant. "I have experiences as well," I explained if I am reading scriptures and I feel the warm presence of the Holy Spirit while reading that means, the scripture and verse or verses you are reading at that time and moment is meant for you. This can happen with your Bible, Inspirational books, read signs or watching ministers on television, there are so many ways the Lord will communicate with you. What is very important, have a notepad even at your bedside to make notes on scripture or a word the Lord will bring you. This is your beginning of growing in this newness of the Lord and his presence making you aware of His presence, communicating instruction of corrections, encouraging you that you are in the right place with Him. You will need to communicate this information to your pastor or family members that are well based in the Word, they can begin to help you understand what the Lord is saying too you. When you are reading your Word, you will encounter in the scripture the Holy Spirit will teach you all things.

Since then, he and I have been in constant contact, I been led by the Holy Spirit to pray blessing in his life, and learn to trust the Lord. I wasn't certain then nor

now, I suggested to my young friend, perhaps the Holy Spirit led him to me, so I could share my experiences with him and offer guidance and refer him to someone else so he can continue to grow and draw nearer to the Lord. The Lord wanted you to get it correctly, He often speaks through His vessel that He will trust with His word and your preparation for your calling. I reminded him there will be trials and tribulation as he is developed and shaped into a vessel as a child of the Most High.

This morning my young friend called with this interesting story, he met this family at the playground when he was with his daughter. This family talked with him about finding a school for their young child. His daughter's academy is an excellent choice, he recommended the academy, they accepted his suggestion and placed their child in the school.

After they had gone their separate ways, this young soldier felt the presence of the Holy Spirit and knew he had to do something. There were two cultures and religions involved, he wondered which of the parents would be more acceptable to hear his appeal about being a child of the Lord.

He called me, we rationalized the choice, he chose to speak with his wife. I suggested, don't talk to her about her religion or culture. I invited my young friend to prayer, in our prayer I asked the Lord, to speak into our spirit bless us with His Word, and we can avoid all false ways, the way of the Lord is always filled with righteousness. After prayer, I felt in my spirit, tell my friend to share his story, explain who you were at once upon a time, what the Lord has done for you and while you are able to bring your daughter to school and have fun and games in the playground. Many children find their way to Christ through testimonies, when we tell our story, this gives The Holy Spirit the opportunity to bless their lives and enhance there going and resolve perhaps and issues that are already present. I suggested to my young friend, the Holy Spirit often used us in the field where we have our experiences, while establishing your feet, the Holy Spirit is using you to bring another lost sheep out of darkness into His marvelous light, the Lord is the true Shepherd of our lives. While writing this, the Lord dropped this into my spirit. Jeremiah 29:11.

When my friend tells his story, how the Lord fought his battle and delivered his child into his arms, this is why they are together having fun on the playground. He remembered the prayers I continued to pray for him, although your faith wasn't yet strong enough to have the faith and believe Lord would bring resolution into your situation. You trusted our friendship and I trusted what I heard in the spirit realm while fasting, and reading my scriptures, and sharing the situation with our family prayer line with Prophetess Frankie and Evangelist Margaret prayer line.

Translation:

Peter concludes this brief letter as he began, by urging his leaders to grow in the grace and knowledge of the Lord and Savior Jesus Christ, to get to know him better and better. This is the most important steps in refuting false teachers. No matter where we are in our spiritual journey, no matter how mature we are in our faith, the sinful world always will challenge our faith, we will always have room for growth. If every day we find some way to draw closer to Christ, we will be prepared to stand for truth in any and all circumstances.

Chapter Twenty Three

HE IS THE ANSWER

Mark 16:20 (niv) Then the disciples went out and preached everywhere, and the Lord worked with them and confirmed his word by the signs that accompanied it.

I was working at my barn on a Monday morning, when I first heard the name Barack Obama, it was announced that he had thrown his hat into the presidential race. I question to myself, can this guy win the presidency, I heard in my spirit, if he runs, he'll win. Since then, I have great confidence in his ability to lead and to whom he is led by. When many others were frantic with concerns, with the vicious and racially motivated comments from the talk show host, news stations even those that are his

145

counterpart made a racially motivated statement towards his race.

The compassion, the love, and respect this man shows even to those that dislike him for his race, he demonstrates that he is a man of God and doesn't return ugly remarks to those that try to degrade him. The lovely and powerful first lady is equally spiritually fed and led by the Holy Spirit of God, she also is receiving all matter of remarks about there race. They are demonstrating who they are in Christ Jesus and how The President and First Lady of The White House of The United States should present themselves before the people of this country and to other nations. Personally, I don't believe there has been a president and first lady grace the White House as beautifully as the Obama's.

When we are on a mission, that is established by the Holy Spirit, in this situation, he is the President of The United States and he set forth a promise to the American people there is a change, in that change the people would be taken care off before the rich. Our broken educational system, jobs outsource to other countries and change our dependency from totally on oil to other innovated energy sources.

My purpose here is to identify, that we as a people and children's of God, we need to pray for our President and First Lady. They are handicapped in so many ways, I am going to continue to pray and send the Angels of God to cover them. Our Lord promised to take care of those who trust in Him.

Prophetess Frankie has powerful insight, blessed by the Holy Spirit and she sees President Barack grandmother, in her vision and through our prayers, we will send her to him, to be that which he stands in need off. I have prayed that the mighty hand of God continually cover him and protect him from his adversaries, touch hearts and minds that they may be changed and the people may benefit from the government parties working together.

TRANSLATION:

Jesus taught us servanthood, so He went about teaching, preaching that all men would receive his Word. With all His power in heaven and earth, Jesus chose to be a servant. He held children in his arms, and healed the sick, washed the disciples feet, and died for the sins of the world. As believers, we are called to be servants of Christ, as Christ served, so we are to serve.

Chapter Twenty Four

YOU CAN DEPEND ON ME

Psalm 118:24 (niv) this is the day the Lord has made let us rejoice and be glad in it.

Often we encounter issues and situations that are overwhelming to us, we talk to others and we find ourselves unable to find a resolution, it is beyond our reach. We know there is a Higher Power. I will learn to seek the Lord first, I have learned He loves to be consulted first, not just in your trouble time but in all things. My dad, the Reverend Frank says "If we learn this important fact, we serve a jealous God," who sits high and look at his children. Over the years the Lord truth has given me experiences to live by and to tell others about this Lord of our lives.

I have a family friend, his daughter called him with a health issue and with short notice, he couldn't get to be with her in her downtime. He called up his lifelong friend and gave me the assignment to be with her. There is a young man I have lend time to, hoping he would get a good foot hole on life and except a new direction and make some changes for the better. He and I seemed to be in agreement with.

This young friend, I mentor, drove for me, when we arrived at the clinic, I went inside to locate her. I called her cellular number and we talked. I looked around she was sitting across from me with her best friend. Although she was on staff at the clinic, her name was listed late for a procedure and would probably wait three to four hours. At that moment I felt the desire to pray for the Lord to bless her every need. Lord all her needs are in your hands, I believe you have already accessed her needs and would take care of it, I know my best friend lives in you and have already trusted you with her needs.

After prayer we wiped away a few tears, the spirit was very high and mighty for us and I heard in my spirit "she has favor," the voice in my spirit was so clear, I looked around to see if anyone else heard His voice. How sweet it is. Minutes later the attendant walked up and took her to processing.

I introduced myself to her mister, we were talking, he looked familiar to me although I never seemed him before, the gray scruffy beard on this handsome young man. I asked, "What kind of work you do?" "I am a shapeup brick mason, trying to latch onto a fixed location to start work at every day." I am looking at the mister keenly it seems to me I knew him and the lite gray beard assured me he was the person in the night watch that came into my vision with his wife's face. I didn't know who this couple was, and this wasn't a surprise the Lord brings assignments in the nights watch on occasions and I pray immediately in the Holy Spirit, for he knows what I should pray for.

I called Prophetess Frankie and shared the amazing move of the Lord, He positions me in the night watch with prayer, it seemed for strangers, I am sent with prayers of favor from the Lord, she is immediately processed and two plus hours later work done and cleared to go home. Prophetess Frankie with encouragement promised to lift up the young couple continuingly on our family prayer line for her well being and total healing. We will continue to praise the Lord for His wondrous works, for this is the day the Lord has made let us rejoice and be glad in it. I am home, tired as my mule that I plowed all day back on the farm in the old days, and I get this nudge, and a soft whisper, "Oscar, you didn't pray." It is 1:00 am in the night watch, in my prayer room. I prayed with the fullness of the Holy Spirit for the young couple that I was sent to minister with. As I drifted into sleep and meditation, I hear "tell the young brick mason, ask the Lord for what he wants, and He would do it.

I called the young brick mason later that day, inquired of his wife and informed him "There is a Word from the Lord, you have found favor from the Lord, He says, ask me what you want and I will do it." When we hear from the Lord in this manner, start shouting and celebrate His Holy and precious Name.

TRANSLATION:

There are days when the last thing we want to do is rejoice. Our mood is down, our situation is out of hand and our sorrow or guilt is overwhelming. We are, to be honest with God as we talked to Him, and we will always praise Him. When we don't feel like praising the Lord, talk with Him and He will give us a reason to praise.

Chapter Twenty Five

WE CAN BE CHANGED

Matthew 3:8 (niv) Produce fruit in keeping with repentance.

I have been talking with a young man, he was thin and had a searching look about himself. We opened with prayer, I always like to give the day to the Lord, I need His covering for safety of the work and workers, unseen dangers and snares we pray for safety in Jesus name. I assigned him work and demonstrated how the work should be done. Since then, I have made a conscious effort to try and establish a relationship with my new friend. When he works, he wants good direction and understanding that the work done on the property was done professionally. I let him know that will come with training and his desire to learn.

He shared interesting information about himself, he talked about his past and admitted he is stubborn sometimes and even more so when he is pushed unnecessarily. I was so appreciated for his openness. I suggested to him, these kinds of situation don't sneak up on you. I suggested through your prayers, reading and studying the Bible and attending a good Bible-based church and sharing with the pastor you can outgrow your circumstances that delay your growth and maturing. The company you keep will quickly improve when you move from the street corners to your local church. It is important when you want to have a clear understanding of how to move forward. My young friend was speaking about spiritual growth and a good understanding that he is reliable and dependable in what he say and do.

Coming into Thanksgiving, he was hired to work at a factory and from what I understand, he did well and is interviewed to be called for another work. Surely our

Lord is our "Great Teacher," We Can Be Changed, this is why He came to help us get it right.

My great concern in sharing this story, it is so familiar, how so many of our young people are searching for direction. Naturally, we can't understand their past, we meet our young men and women where they are and try with patience to share our experiences. I shared some failures that I been falling down and getting up all my life. and explain that our parents were tremendous support, and taught us with loving patience but didn't spare the rod and spoil a child. I speak clearly to our youth, they must be able to follow instructions, and not be afraid to learn from their mistakes.

We as parents are wearing out our knees before the master, to cover our young loved ones, protect them from themselves, O' Lord guard their stumbling feet from hurt harm and danger until they're ready to give their lives for you. I am mindful that myself and others are still trying to get it right with the Lord. This is not to condemn, we all need to pull together and try and help save our youth and we can witness together the rebuilding of the Kingdom of God. To identify the problem, one would think everybody knows what our children are doing, what is the resolve, we must go back to the days when we grew up, we are now in our seventies and sixties, but in the day we were governed by the community. Each parent had the assignment to correct another parent's child, up to and including discipline. We are fighting for our very lives now, we need to protect the generation to come, we have lost two generation of our sons and daughters already thru incarceration, drugs and gun violence at alarming numbers.

We as the community need more programs, job fairs and the parents need to acknowledge that by ourselves we can't save our children, if the community comes together we have many eyes to see the goings and coming of our children. I wish love would fall in our community so we can reconnect with each other. Thru prayer, fasting and studying our scriptures, beseeching the Lord to draw us and protect our youth, dear heavenly father, protect our remnant with your righteous hand, Lord God Almighty. "We Can Be Changed."

TRANSLATION:

Words and rituals will not produce fruit, in keeping with repentance, this means God looks beyond our words and religious activities to see if our conduct backs up what we say, and he judges our words by the actions that accompany them.

Chapter Twenty Six

OBEDIENCE

Luke 9:62 (Niv) Jesus replied, "No one who puts his hand to the plow and look back is fit for service in the kingdom of God.

Early this morning, the prayer team were intercessors for others, and there were praise reports that went out and we were thankful to the Holy Spirit that answers our continued prayer and to God be the Glory and Praise.

Evangelist Margaret was prophetic and spoke to expectancy for 2011 with the move of the Lord, moving in the midst of our team we can expect assignments trends to lead us to increase our study of the scripture, increase in prayer and fasting.

As Evangelist Margaret prophesy, I made notes, I am frightened when I hear prophesy coming from the Lord, through his Evangelist. The Lord gave her a word to establish a prayer line in 2002 and it has been a powerful blessing through many years to many people, even today in 2018.

She always speaks with authority, as if the very words are coming from on High, from the mouth of the Lord, "You are the apple of my eye," I was very surprise to hear that on our prayer time. She goes on to say, He sees a pillar in you, you are to stay energized, places to go, keep a full tank and be ready to go for Him. Servants are those who say yes to the Lord Jesus Christ and are willing to trust Him. He leads us and covers us on our going out and coming in. Receiving that from the Evangelist were complete because I had read it in the scripture while reading and was convicted to tears in Zechariah 3:8.

I said in my spirit, I am the guy, that didn't yield to my calling for many years when I finally said yes, I was in my early sixties. Evangelist Margaret, gave me one of her favorite scriptures to support me and stay encouraged. Trust in the Lord with all thine heart; and lean not unto thine own understanding. In all thy ways acknowledge him, and he shall direct your paths. Proverb 3:5-6.

TRANSLATION:

No one can do any business in a proper manner if he is attending to other things. Those who begin with the work of God must resolve to go on, or they will make nothing of it. Looking back leads to drawing back, and drawing back is to perdition. He only that endures to the end shall be saved.

Chapter Twenty Seven

SWEETER THAN A HONEYCOMB

Psalm 119:103 (niv) How sweet are your words to taste, sweeter than honey to my mouth!

Late this evening, I was moved to do my visit at the care facility. On my last visit, there was a friend that I had prayed for with the family members that were present and takes great care of their mother. She had lost her appetite and much prayer had gone up for her. On the previous prayer, a word from the Holy Ghost came out while I was praying, the word said her food would come to taste like that of a sweet honeycomb. I blessed His word, I had just received and the Holy Ghost presence was very strong and surely all the glory, honor and praise goes to the Holy Ghost who answer our prayers. Going to the care facility five o'clock in the evening is usually late for me, the thought would not leave me alone, so with the wet dreary cold weather before me, I went over and began my visits. As I came through the front entrance my visit became worthwhile. I was glad I came, there was the system operator there and I hadn't seen her in months. I went to the window and told her I had prayed for her a number of times and wondered how she was doing. She works night, with that I wouldn't see her.

I said to her "If it were permitted, I'll come

in there and hug you," she said," I can come out". She greeted me with a hug and I wished her continued blessings. She spoke what I believe a word from the Holy Ghost, she said the Lord is going to restore back to me all that has been stolen from me, in my kindness, His will is to do so, Hallelujah, thank you, Christ Jesus.

My friend, I was in excellent spirit now that I had seen the system operator. I sent powerful prayers to her and the Holy Spirit have spoken to her needs and we have shared tears in the midst of our prayers, thanking the Lord for what He was doing in our lives. On the floor I saw my friend that had very little appetite was resting well and looked refreshed. I came over to the bedside and greeted her and she spoke and raised her hands to shake mine, she was eating again in her nineties.

Coming of the elevator, a visitor looked at me and saw I was the volunteer Chaplin on that floor, she said her mother were in the next bedroom, after coming into the room, I realize why the visitor lady had invited me to her mother's bed side for prayer. She had been present doing our prayers and saw the work of the Holy Ghost for herself on our patient without the appetite. I came to her mother and had prayer with her as well. We also became friends.

The system operator blessed me with strong prayers. There were times I kept my appointments for the guest although I didn't feel well. She tells me, she had a word from the Lord, He would bless me with utterance, this would support my ministry. I was thankful for the gift of utterance, this was my second time receiving this prophecy and scripture.

TRANSLATION:

God's Word makes us wise; wiser than our enemies and wiser than any teachers who ignore it. True wisdom goes beyond amassing knowledge: it is applying knowledge in a life-changing way. Wisdom comes from allowing what God teaches to guide us.

Chapter Twenty Eight

A TOUCH FROM HIS HAND

Psalm :91:15 (kjv) He shall call upon me,
   and I will answer him: I will be with him in
   trouble; I will deliver him, and honor him.

Tuesday night, I received a call from my friend,
that her Uncle, was put in the hospital critically
ill. With weakened lungs on Sunday, she called
me Tuesday night and reviewed the events that
are against them in the family and they need
support and prayer.

Briefly, she said they just had the homecoming for her uncle from 2011. This uncle's issue this Sunday night had her continually in prayer and asking for more help in these storm of life that is raging in her family right now, I recall. Earlier in the year, she lost her best friend. We can't explain life stories, they're our testimonies that the Holy Spirit lay on our heart and we tell them that they may be a beacon of hope for others, to know the Holy Spirit is our ever-present help and He touches us with His powerful hand, bringing hope and peace to the wounded children that are His creation.

In my prayer with my friend, I called for the righteous hand of my heavenly Father to send His healing angel to her uncle's bedside, I asked for His most powerful healing angel that's in the presence of the Lord and to send Raphael with His angel and the healing touch. When I wrote this I felt the Holy Spirit so strongly it brought me to tears, that His loving touch is enough and I confess, I love the Holy Spirit for answer prayers of so many who are praying for this blessing.

My friend this evening brought good news, that her uncle was out of serious danger, her family member for the first time since her best friend pass this summer she showed improvement. Since her lost, she wavered some the mother seemed to be in this unhealthy state until today when they shared the improved condition of my friend's uncle, her brother-in-law. Her mother seemed to have rebounded to her regular self. When the Holy Spirit is touching and releasing healing for the family also receive what the spirit has far us.

TRANSLATION:

We will learn when we are in great need of the covering of God, His mighty healing and the righteous arm of protection from the Lord, we are to realize, that which we pray for must be in right alignment with the will of the Lord. If we trust in the Lord, His will, will be done, and we have his secured covering through now and eternity.

Chapter Twenty Nine

A BURDEN BARRRIER

Psalm 55:22 (niv) cast your cares on the Lord and he will sustain you, he will never let the righteous fall.

I called a friend, to offer her support from my wife and myself, she was preparing to leave on a mission trip. I admire others that give of themselves to go and make sacrifices for the benefits of others, they have my total respect and prayers, for the Holy Spirit to cover them and guard their feet in their travel on missions to support others.

While on the telephone, agreeing on a location to meet, I felt a tremendous heaviness from her and I was getting a feeling she needs help and I asked her to share with me what was happening with her. I explained that she didn't know me very well, but the Lord has blessed me with a ministry and she can trust me in confidence.

She explained, a family member had gotten involved in a personal matter, and it must get resolved, and we need prayer. I remember saying to her, the burden isn't hers to carry, I reminded her, we can go to the Lord and tell Him what we need, and He will bless you, He can hold a situation in place and answer your prayers. Our Lord is a burden barrier we can trust Him and give all our cares to the Lord. Always remember family, our Lord is our first prayer, through faith our first line of defense, and our Good Shepherd, He never leaves His children that trust Him nor those who are learning to trust him.

My wife and I met her with the promised support for the mission that were coming soon then I offer her prayer, in my spirit I felt the presence of the Holy Spirit, he gave me a name, I thought it was just my thinking, and I heard the name again, I called Prophetess Frankie, a powerful prayer intercessor for the righteous, I heard your name in my spirit so I called you, there is a new friend needs family prayer. You are our prayer team leader, so I call so we can enlist others on the team and bring this prayer request continually before the Lord.

I am pending this testimony hoping that those who read this testimony will know that our Lord and Savior hears our prayers, He is our burden barrier, His yoke is light, surely he will bear our burdens, and sustains us in this hour of need. When the prayer ended we thank the Holy Spirit for lifting the burden of his beloved daughter, we are believing the Lord has this situation in hand and the problem would be resolved according to His will. This young man must prepare for tuff love, and learn how to serve the Lord.

We call for prayer again that night with others of the prayer team that has been interceding for others for years. We praise the Lord and thank Him for coming in a hurry to lift our burden, giving us the strength to run this race, that we identify as our mission work. Since this young man had this encounter, on my follow-up, I heard this young man has turned his life towards the Lord. To God be the glory and all the praise.

Our take away family, when life situations seem to crush us from every side, don't give up, and don't give in. Somewhere in your family lineage, a family member, a church pastor must have talked about the Lord and His saving grace. Anyone who feels trapped and in a dark room and feel like there is no way out, open the window blinds and open the doors and let the bright light of the Lord shine on you. The Lord will knock on the

doors of your heart, but you must let Him in.
Thank you Lord for saving me.

TRANSLATION: PSALMS (niv) 55:22

God wants us to cast our cares on him, but often we continue to bear them ourselves even when we say we are trusting in him. Trust the same strength that sustains you to carry your cares also.

Chapter Thirty

BE WILLING TO SERVE

I PETER 4:11; (niv) As every man hath received the gift, even so minister the same one to another, as good stewards of the manifold grace of God.

My friend invited me this Friday to come with him and inspect a potential building that he would like to relocate his tour bus company to. He would need a location that would allow interior parking under lock and key and out of the visible scrutiny of vandals and bad weather.

My desire on the way to the facility was to invite the Holy Spirit to come with me and help me to know the things, that I wouldn't ordinarily know. We arrived and met the owner. He showed us the building

and the offices, which would more than supply our needs and a couple additional small owners. We looked and walked the facility and it were more than adequate. This is a previous facility that was used for buses to be dispatched and the issues that were before us. I hadn't felt the unction of the Holy Spirit and I am saying to myself the spirit didn't speak to this. Also, they would be willing to build a new office and interior parking location to accommodate interior parking and with this, the rental fee goes up additional fifteen hundred dollars with a lock-in five year lease that would cost enough to buy or build his own facility.

I said to my friend, I hadn't felt the presence of the Holy Spirit, I think He is telling us, He wants to provide us with ownership, not paying someone else to rent. I made these comments while preparing to leave for home.

Before we left and I was sitting in one of the comfortable high back office chairs the owner was talking to Marvin about office filing cabinets that he wants him to order for him. While they were talking, I felt the presence of the Holy Spirit and I asked if someone were praying about something because I felt

Him in our presence. Each said they hadn't and as they were saying know. I felt the prompting a second time and I said I just felt his presence again. Owner said it must be the spirit on him because he had and unusual incident that transpired and only the Holy Spirit could have done this. He was in a hurry, drove up quickly, exited his car and looked back. The car was driving straight ahead and went between two brand new buses and didn't scratch either one. He declared the Lord was driving the car and when the car hit the fence and got only a few scratches on the front bumper, he said that was the Lord, that is why he said I felt the presence of the Holy Spirit on him.

When I was leaving the property, I said to myself when I feel the prompting of the Holy Spirit I usually need to pray for someone. We prayed with the belief that I knew the Holy Spirit will answer the prayer and tend to the needs of the intended. The presence of the Holy Spirit was awesome and I felt fulfilling of our needs. When I was about to leave, the owner came up to my car and said, Sir, will you pray for my mother? She had issues over two years ago and is doing alright, be confident the Lord answers prayer.

TRANSLATION:

Our abilities should be faithfully used in serving others; none are for our own exclusive enjoyment. Some people, well aware of their abilities, believe that they have the right to used their abilities as they please. Others think they have no gifts, find your gift and used them, we all are blessed by God with gifts, to fulfill His purpose in our lives.

Chapter Thirty One

HOLD ON TO YOUR FAITH

Psalm 91:1 (niv) He who dwells in the shelter of the Most High will rest in the shadow of the Almighty.

This morning, I received a call from my friend, she wanted to share a special blessing that her son had experienced a stranger who saw him walking by, called him over and said, I need prayer for my daughter who is sick in the Medical Center. Her son has a blessed calling on his life, this was not so unusually being called upon for prayer by strangers.

After the prayers and the presence of the Holy Spirit were very presence, her son was able to say to the lady, I believe the Lord answered your prayer your daughter will be well. When I received this testimony I felt the prompting of the Holy Spirit very strongly and I may have misjudged the presence of the Holy Spirit I felt His prompting my dear friend name came to mind, I believe that was my answer also, she was well.

She's working in a facility, and something there seems to aggravate her and in a few days she doesn't feel well. We desired the Lord bless her in her situation until there is another remedy. The prayer team has been lifting her up while she is recovering through prayer.

When I received the unction of the Holy Spirit, I believed also it was my answer as well because the lady saw the prayer warrior again shortly after, said she had spoken with her daughter and she is doing well. I have prayed and believed she would be well in the name of our Lord and Savior from our prayer team and others, and my personal prayers.

We can witness, how we held onto our faith by trusting the Holy Spirit for the answer to our prayers. I believe this lady prayers was so faithful to trust the Holy Spirit that, He set her in the right place and call on a servant that would hear and obey and would allow the Holy Spirit to fulfill the need for the prayerful mother and the Father would get the Glory. The Holy Spirit affirmed the blessing on the mother's daughter by sending the praying servant by a location where she would see him and give thanks, she has heard the daughter is doing well. The happy mother got the news from the praying servant, her son and she calls her brother to share the good news of God and the Holy Spirit speaks.

Our blessing is dependent on our faithfulness and trust in the Lord. We are the commission the Lord created us to be. We are the Great

Commission and if we follow the leading and guidance of the Lord, we will be in the right places to minister the gospel of Jesus Christ.

TRANSLATION

God is a shelter, a refuge when we are afraid.
David faith was in the Almighty God as
Protector would carry him through all the
dangers and fears of life. This should be a
picture of our trust-trading all our fears for
faith in him, no matters how intense our fears.
We are to entrust ourselves to his protection
and pledging our daily devotion to him, we will
be kept safe.

Chapter Thirty Two

BE FIRM WITH ME

Psalm 118:8 (niv) It is better to take refuge in the Lord than to trust man.

There is a young man I been trying to mentor with and introduce him to work ethics and responsibility that come with preparedness for work assignments. Most of the time he and I, his brother didn't agree. Loose baggie pants, no belts and not keeping time commitments are instruments of failure. I am rather firm on commitments, I try to explain that very fact. They agree with the explanation of accountability, but need more work and training through the patience of the Holy Spirit gives me. I. confess I need to seek forgiveness before the day is over, in the event I speak firm or say too much.

In recent months, there are mark improvements in younger brother attitude and work ethics. I remember a few weeks before today, I was talking with him and he said something very profound. He called and thank me for working with him and suggested that I don't let up, stay firm on him because he needed it. I need to explain sometimes that I am too hard on them and I need to apologize, he said "Popper Senior, you are teaching me to be a man." He then asked for prayer because he was going to apply Monday for a job and he wanted to be blessed and feel confident.

Today, he called and asked for work until his final test comes in from the job interview, I directed him to the correct person for available work. While we were talking, I thought I felt the prompting of the Holy Spirit to pray, I then invited this young into prayer so the Holy Spirit would bless him, according to what the will of God is.

While pending this, I asked of the Holy Spirit to bless me with right thought, place my sight on the right information, notes of excellent recall that the presence of the Holy Spirit would be in this work and lesser of me. When others read our testimonies they to will be touched by the Holy Spirit and find hope. I confess, when I completed this, the Holy Spirit came upon me and filled me with tears. Family, I am trying to get it right with the Lord, so He can trust me more. If we stay in Him, we won't stay in the same places for the Lord will grow us. When the Lord gets a willing spirit, He is "Firm with Us," so we can grow to our full potential.

This young man and I prayed for his job and he hasn't been without a job for over four years. Our God is a keeper for those who diligently seek him.

TRANSLATION

Each day we must put our confidence in trains, cars, or buses. Each day we must put our confidence in something or someone. If you are willing to trust a plane or car to reach a destination. Are we willing to trust God to guide us here on earth and to our eternal destination? I hope we don't trust the material things of the world more than we trust the Lord. The Lord is our ever-present help, we must trust him with all that we have.

Chapter Thirty Three

I AM BIRTHING YOU

Psalms (niv.) 62:11-12; One thing God has spoken,
two things I have heard: "Power belongs to you, God,
(vs.12) and with you, Lord, is unfailing love," and,
"You reward everyone according to what they have
done.

There was a property needing major overhauling and
is now in progress. The owner prayed, asked the Lord
for the right company to get the job and attend
personally to its completion, from personal knowledge
the owner has sensed from previous properties were
butchered by tree companies. They agree to what you
say, and take the premium trees and leave the property

torn up with damages, tree stumps and branches. The contractors fail to clear the property forcing the

customer, to hire someone else for the final clearance and leave the property in decent and in order as the Lord would have it. I Corinthians 14:40; But let all things be done decently and in order.

The owner was rationalizing over a short list of tree companies and hadn't dial a single number, because he was not comfortable in his gut with what he had. He tells his story about sitting at his desk, not even thinking of a tree company, this name drops into his spirit and he smiles and made the call. He remembered there was a previous emergency tree work done by this young minister after a terrible storm. The dangerous work was done and the cleanup was excellent. Be diligent to the search and believe that which you have prayed for you will receive, Sweet Jesus, and Darling Holy Ghost, I bless your name with glory and honor, for the answered prayer. He answered with a hello, the owner explained the tree work and invited the minister out for a price quote at the new location. The young minister moved with authority through the requested removal site and established rules to be applied with the removing all the trees designated, branches and debris, the owner replied to himself this sounds like the right plan, thank you Lord for blessing your servant.

I have seen and done a great deal of trees removal myself, watching these young men with such precision, gave me new insight and appreciation for this new breed of men coming alone in today's job market. The owner commented the men arrived early every day and go right to their assignments without their leader being present. The devil is a liar, our young men are proud of their heritage and have a willingness to work to support self and their families. The enemy throws a rock and hide their hands, this means the rich send the jobs overseas for greater profits and point at the jobless and call them lazy and unwilling to work. The work is very hard and dangerous as well, the workers move forward with caution and safety was their first priority. Each worker is getting ready to drop down a tree, he locates each partner then send the tree to the ground. The tree removal was going very well, the bobcat rolled over something and gave it a flat. They checked the owner for the nearest purchase of a tube and repair. The purchase and repair was a minimum two-hour turnaround. After the flat tire, things got crazy, a small oil leak became bigger each day and it slowed the work pace. I admired the young minister how he tends to the task as a mechanic on his equipment, making repairs and continue to work. He lost a few days with the oil leak but was in good form to finish up. The young minister once again in full speed to get the job done, and the hydraulics fail to open and closed consistently then they stopped functioning altogether and a mechanic was brought in.

The roadside mechanic traced, tested, and couldn't get the hydraulics to work at all. The owner went down to inquire about their progress and he saw the mechanic stressed and pressed what should he do next. The owner said to the Lord, the young minister doesn't want to be under this shade tree not working and the owner doesn't want to see him under this shade tree not working and you Lord sent him here to work the job to completion, so whisper a word for the mechanic so he can make the repair. At that very moment, the owner heard in the spirit, a hydraulic valve is locked and won't open, it may be bad. The mechanic heard that and immediately started testing circuits to see where was the power cut off. The young minister calls the owner and thanked him for the word the Lord gave for the mechanic to make the repair. A valve was bad the mechanic bypassed the valve with a straight wire. Doing this exchange with the owner, the Lord had a word for the young minister. The breakdowns occurred and the Lord turned them into a test. He wanted an outward showing of your characters, be more like Christ.

The Lord said you handle the emergencies with an excellent temperament your attitude towards the owner and workers, you were attentive to commitment, you showed your obedience to commitment, you had a backup plan, you ordered in additional bobcat loader, extra dumpster, the cost wasn't the issue at this point. The young ministers were greatly concerned, he had made a promise, his name is attached to it, he desires to stand proudly before the Lord he serves

The Lord wanted to see if you could stand when your equipment was falling apart all around you, work all day very long hours, and drive hours away the same day and preached revival for four nights. "The Lord Said, "I Am Birthing You," for new heights in my name. I speak blessings over your life with authority from on high, to the Lord be the glory

TRANSLATION

God hath spoken as it were once for all, the power belongs to him alone. He can punish and destroy. Mercy also belongs to him; and his recompensing the imperfect services of those that believe in him, blotting out their transgressions for the Redeemer's sake, is a proof of abundant mercy, and encourages us to trust in him. Let us trust in his mercy and grace, and abound in his work, expecting mercies from him alone.

ABOUT THE AUTHOR

Oscar Dixon, Sr.

I was born in Roba, Alabama, August 29, 1942, to Ethel and Rev. Frank D. Dixon, he was a pastor in the Alabama A. M. E. Zion Church Conference. I gave my life to Christ at a very early age, about ten or eleven years old, and were baptized and joined The County Line A. M. E. Zion Church, under the pastorate of Reverend Robert Day.

Through prayer and fasting, I learned, I was called into the ministry at the tender age of fourteen by our Lord, Jesus Christ. As I grew up, I had many encounters from my youth to adulthood, my parents, explained these events, and finally they said we were peculiar children.

211

I am married, to Mrs. Gloria Allen Dixon, for over 53 years with two children, Oscar Lee and Melinda Rae Dixon Chapman. We are grandparents to Oscar Narjee and Natosha Dixon Porter, who gives us two great grands, Imani and Zechariah.

When the Lord called me this time, he got my attention, I had retired from my job, and was in my late fifties. I had built houses and was renovating properties. Doing this time, I became very sick and, I didn't feel so deserving, but the Lord turned my fears into joy. My church family new of my struggles with my health and they prayed without ceasing, I remember my pastor saying to me brother Oscar we are praying for you. Why working on my property, the Lord call my name, He asked me "Will You Serve Me," I said yes and I have not looked back, but sought every opportunity to prepare myself to be able to serve. I took my theology studies from Beacon University,

Columbus, Georgia, I achieved my Associate Degree, and Bachelors Degree of Theology. From the Christian Life Studies of Theology, I achieved my Master's Degree of Theology in 2013. I have three years in the The African Methodist Episcopal Zion Church studies.

In 2005, I was invited to come on a mission trip into downtown Atlanta, I am still here working in 2017. I volunteered to work in two health and rehabilitation facility, I began in 2007 and 2008. There is a take away in this spiritual focus, remember when you pray, believe what you have prayed for, and receive it has thought it has already manifested itself, because

The Lord answers prayers.